MW01098746

The Whalers

For the people of the south coast ~ Bronwyn

Angus&Robertson
An imprint of HarperCollins*Children's Books*, Australia

First published in Australia in *The Nearest the White Man Gets*
by Hale & Iremonger in 1989
Angus & Robertson edition first published in 1996
This edition published in 1997
by HarperCollins*Publishers* Australia Pty Limited
ABN 36 009 913 517
harpercollins.com.au

Poem collected from Percy Mumbulla by Roland Robinson
Text copyright © The Estate of the late Roland Robinson 1989, 1996
Illustrations copyright © Bronwyn Bancroft 1996

This work is copyright. Apart from any use as permitted under the
Copyright Act 1968, no part may be reproduced, copied, scanned, stored
in a retrieval system, recorded, or transmitted, in any form or by any
means, without the prior written permission of the publisher.

HarperCollins*Publishers*
Level 13, 201 Elizabeth Street, Sydney NSW 2000, Australia
Unit D1, 63 Apollo Drive, Rosedale, Auckland 0632, New Zealand

ISBN 978 0 7322 9531 8

The Australian Children's Classics logo designed by Matt Stanton
Colour reproduction by Graphic Print Group, South Australia
Printed and bound in China by RR Donnelley

6 5 4 3   17 18 19

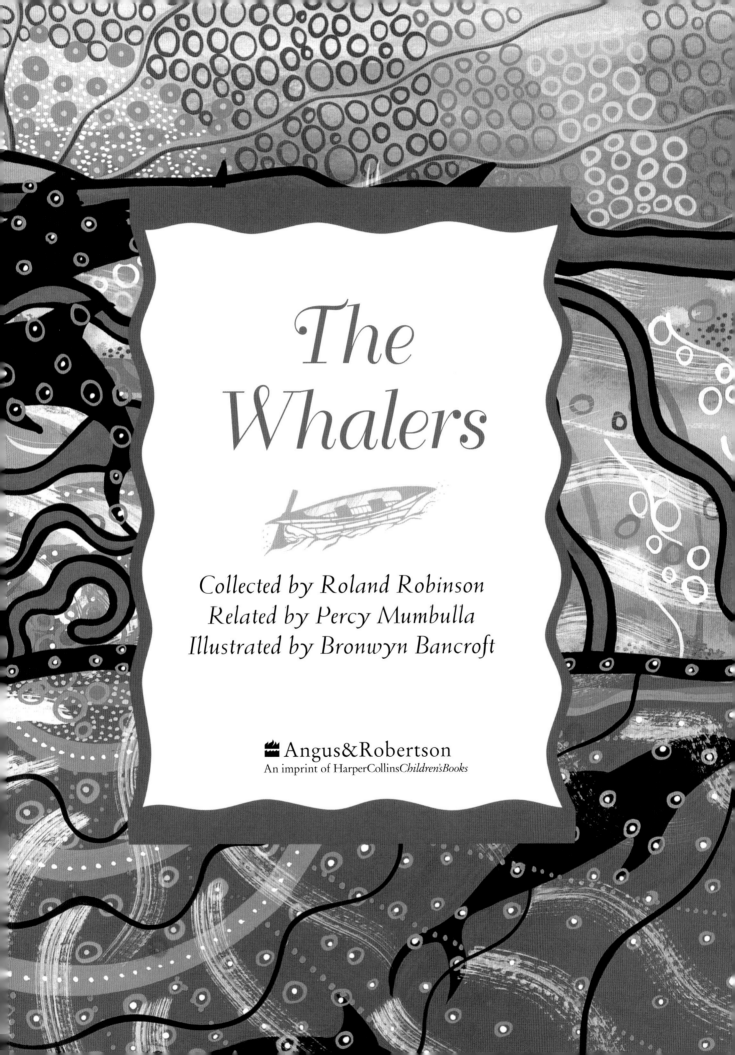

The Whalers

Collected by Roland Robinson
Related by Percy Mumbulla
Illustrated by Bronwyn Bancroft

Angus&Robertson
An imprint of HarperCollins*Children's*Books

✦ FOREWORD ✦

*The Umbara Cultural Centre
is pleased to contribute a
Foreword to* The Whalers

Uncle Percy Mumbulla was a great
storyteller and an important Elder of the
far south coast Aboriginal community. The
Umbara Centre is dedicated to maintaining
and fostering Aboriginal cultures on the
south coast and to making all Australians
more aware of Aboriginal culture, history
and experience.

The Whalers is an important story about
Aboriginal experience on the far south
coast of New South Wales; about our
people's involvement in the whaling
industry, one of the most important
industries in southern Australia from the
beginning of European settlement until

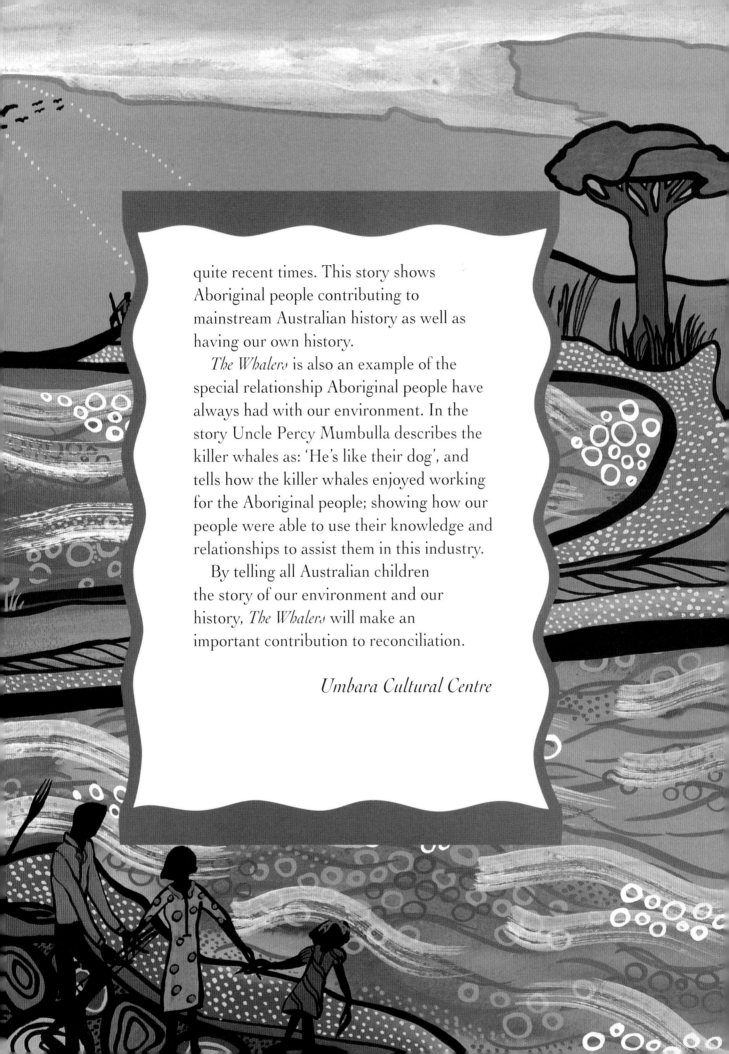

quite recent times. This story shows Aboriginal people contributing to mainstream Australian history as well as having our own history.

The Whalers is also an example of the special relationship Aboriginal people have always had with our environment. In the story Uncle Percy Mumbulla describes the killer whales as: 'He's like their dog', and tells how the killer whales enjoyed working for the Aboriginal people; showing how our people were able to use their knowledge and relationships to assist them in this industry.

By telling all Australian children the story of our environment and our history, *The Whalers* will make an important contribution to reconciliation.

Umbara Cultural Centre

✧ THE WHALERS ✧

My ole Uncle Brierly was the best whaler that ever
they seen in Twofold Bay. One mornin' they was
cuttin' up a whale, an' a killer whale came up
to where they were cuttin' up and jumped straight out
of the water an' splashed his tail, 'Pook-urr', on the water.

Soon as ever he seen this, ole Uncle sings out,
'*Reesh O.*' All the dark fellers run down an' jumped
into the whale-boat, all rowin' their hardest at
the big oars, great big long paddles. The killers was
swimmin' over one another, under and over
backwards an' forwards in front of the whale-boat, playin'.

They gets out an' sees the whale. Ole Uncle sings out, *'Stern-a-moo!'* That means you have to get side on to the whale. Ole Uncle gets the harpoon an' 'Boong!' The harpoon goes into that monster an' kills him stone dead.

They towin' him in now, the killers swimming alongside, playin' with the whale. The killers get real glad whenever they see the dark fellers killin' a whale.

They comin' into the whalin' station now. They goin' to chop the whale up an' boil him. They chuck a big lump of blubber to the killer. He's like their dog.

The dark people would never go lookin' for whales. The killers
would let them know if there were whales about.
Ole Uncle would speak to them killers in the language.
They must have been *bugeens*, clever blackfellers.
They'd go as far as Narooma lookin' for whales.
Two would stop with the whale and one would go back
to Twofold Bay an' leap out of the water. 'Pook-urr!'
He'd slap his tail an' let the whalers know.

The killers would only tell the dark people.
The white people had to look for whales themselves.
It might be the middle of the night when the killers came.
You had no time to look for your trousers or shirt.
When ole Uncle sang out, *'Reesh O!'* you had to run
an' pile into that boat an' out. No matter
if the waves were as high as them trees,
you still had to go because you were signed on.

No shark would touch you with them killers there.
The killers would chop a shark to pieces. A sword-fish,
you know what he's like, he wouldn't have a chance.
An' a porpoise, he'd make a porpoise sweat he's so fast.

If the whale-boat was out of sight of land an' got
smashed, the killers was there. They would
be swimmin' round an' round, keepin' the sharks away.
If them killers seen a man gettin' tired, they would
swim underneath him, put a fin under his arm an'
hold him up until the launch came to pick him up.

The killers would be playin' all around the launch goin' back.

Arr, my old Uncle Brierly was a champ. They've got
his photo down at Twofold Bay. He'd never use
the harpoon-gun. He'd use the harpoon-spear.
He had a knack of killin' the whale, he'd put the harpoon
right into him an' kill the whale stone dead.

There's three whales, the sperm whale, the black whale, an' the humper. A sperm whale can smash a boat with his tail, an' come at you with his mouth open. He's got teeth.

The little killer would swim alongside the whale an' soon as he opened his mouth, the little killer would go inside and bite his tongue out, chew it right off.

Big Ben the killer was a wizard. Then there was Hookey an' Big Tom. Soon as ever the dark people left Twofold Bay an' come to Wallaga Lake, them killers went north, because there were no blackfellers there.

Ole Mrs Davidson, her husband was the boss of the whalin' station at Boyd Town, she could have told you.